THE HUMAN BODY

A MONSTER ACTIVITY BOOK

AUTUMN PUBLISHING

SPOOKY SKELETONS

Beneath your skin, you have a skeleton; a framework of nearly three hundred bones that holds you up and keeps you human-shaped. Without it, your body would be a puddle of soft, squishy organs inside a bag of skin.

Your skeleton

Use your stickers to fill in the gaps on this skeleton.

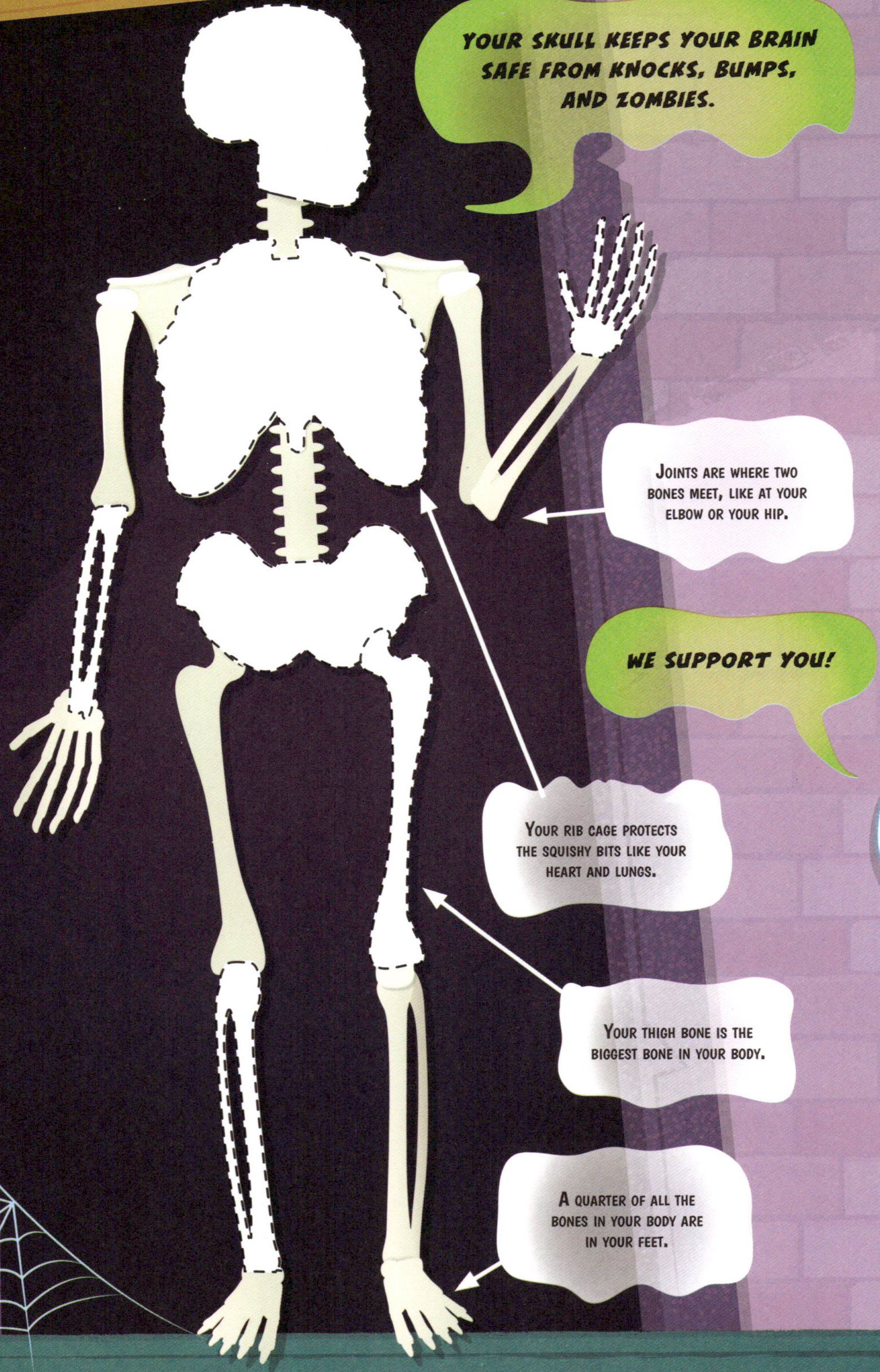

Skeleton Stand

TRY THIS

Stand with your legs straight. Easy. Your weight is being supported by your strong leg bones. Now bend your knees and stay standing. Do your muscles start to ache? This is harder work because your muscles are supporting more of your weight, and they get tired pretty quickly.

Beastly Bones

Bones have to be light, strong, and slightly bendy so they don't snap. Calcium, which you get from drinking milk and eating cheese and nuts, makes your bones strong. Your bones also have something called collagen in them that makes them springy.

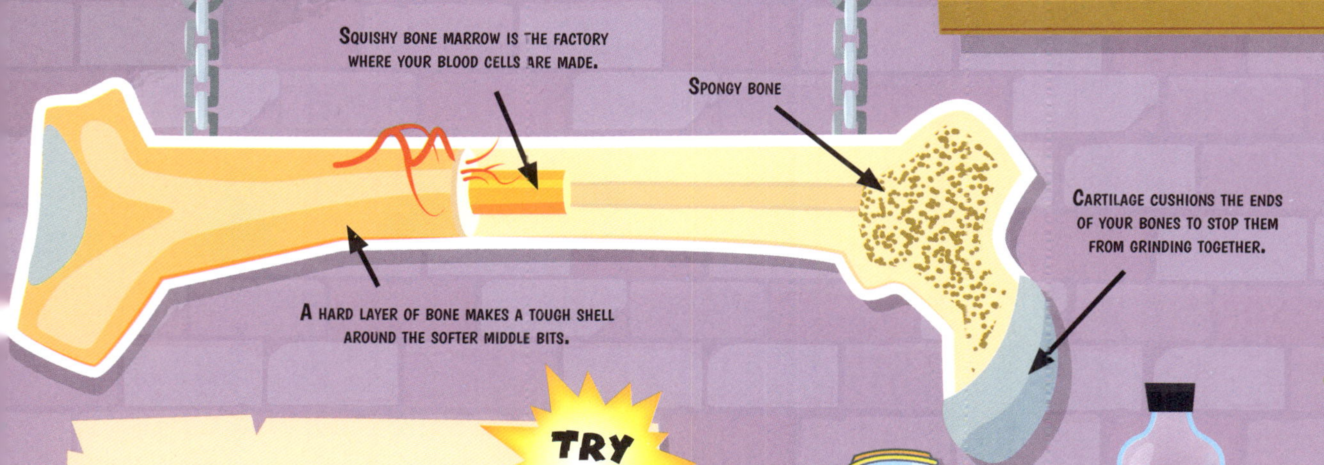

Bendy Bones

TRY THIS

Next time you buy a raw chicken, ask a useful adult to clean a leg bone. Put the bone in a jar filled with vinegar. Screw on the lid and leave it for three days. Then take out the bone and try bending it. The vinegar should have dissolved the calcium in the bone, leaving bendy collagen behind.

WARNING! WASH HANDS THOROUGHLY AFTER TOUCHING RAW MEAT AND BONES!

Brittle Bones

TRY THIS

Ask your useful adult for another clean, uncooked chicken bone. Get them to bake it on a baking tray at 250°F for three hours. When it's cool, carefully try to bend it. The heat should have broken down the collagen, making the bone brittle and easy to snap.

FRANKEN-SKELETON

Now build your own terrifying skeleton using the press-out pieces at the back of the book.

WHY DID THE SKELETON LAUGH?

SOMEONE TICKLED HIS FUNNY BONE.

1 Press out the skull piece. Fold the sides back and slide the tab into the slot. Fold the tabs down around the top of the skull.

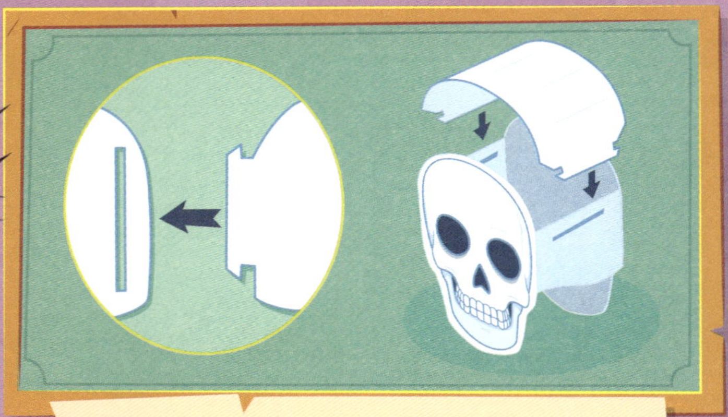

2 Press out the skull top and push the tabs into the slits on either side of the skull so it fits neatly over the folded-down tabs.

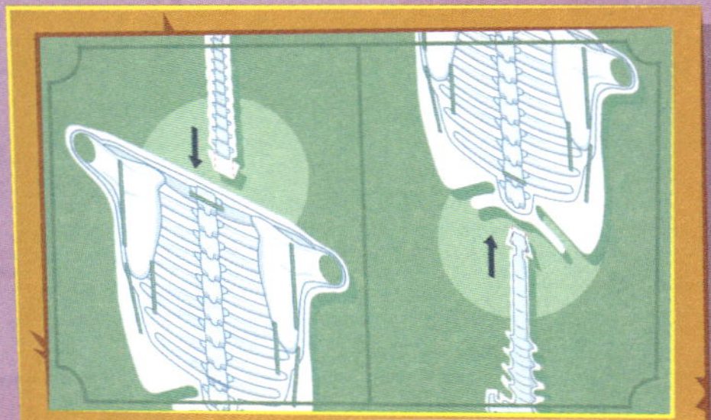

3 Press out the torso and the two spine pieces. Slide the upper spine into the slot at the top of the torso. Slide the lower spine into the slot at the base of the torso.

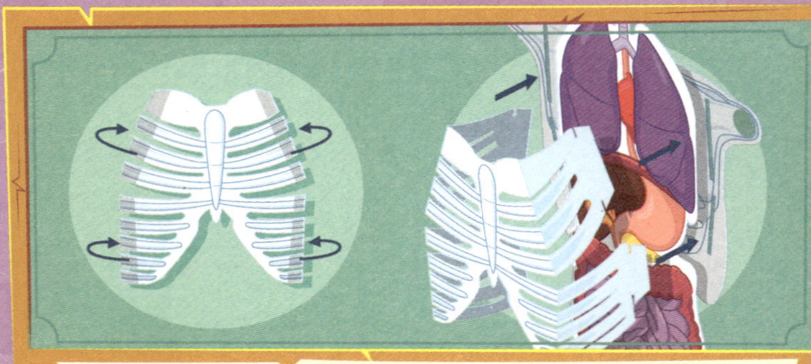

4 Press out the rib cage and the internal organs, folding backward along all the crease lines. Slide the tabs on either side of the internal organs into slots a and b on the torso. Then slide the tabs in the rib cage into slots c, d, e, and f on the torso.

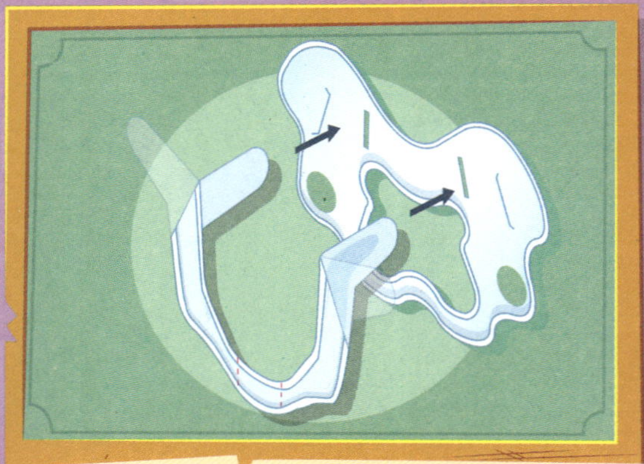

5 Slot the front hip piece into the back hip piece. Then slide the tabs at the bottom of the spine into slots a and b in the back hip piece.

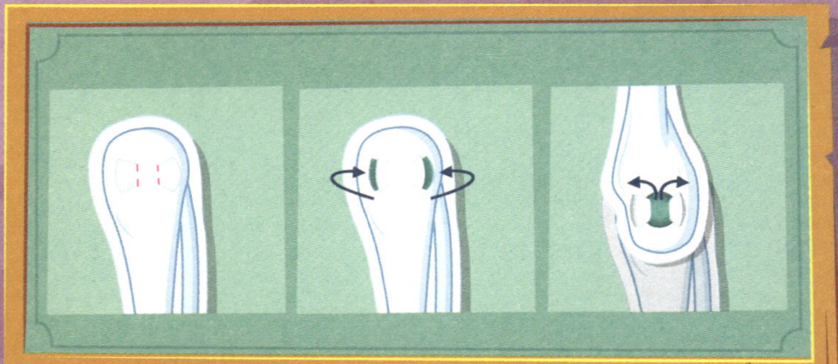

6 Join up the different pieces to make the arms and legs by folding the small tabs upward and slotting them through the circular slot in the connecting piece. Then flatten the tabs back down to secure the joints.

SQUEAK!

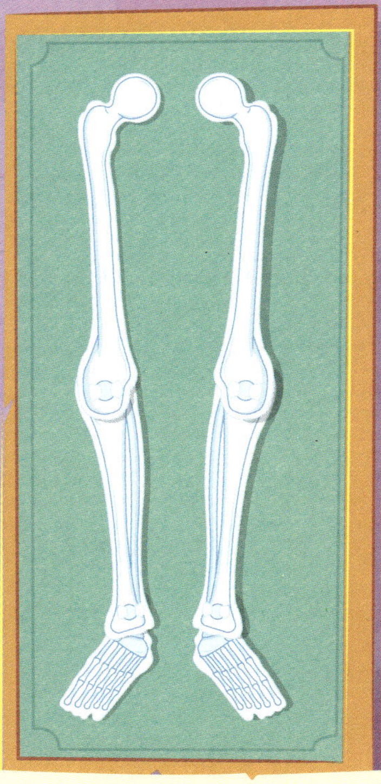

7 Join the right thigh to the right shin, then the right shin to the right foot. Then do the same with the left leg.

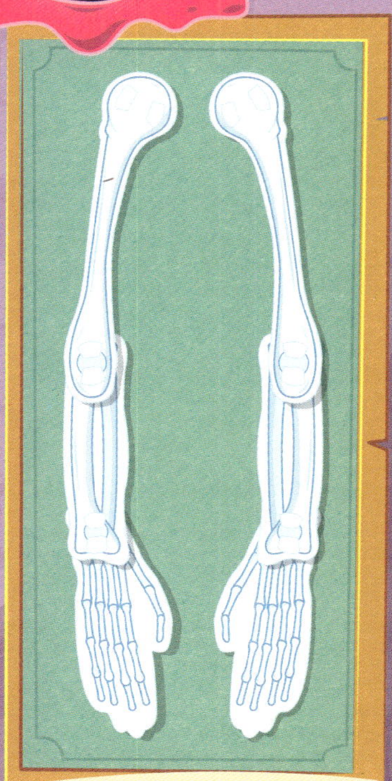

8 Join the right upper arm to the right forearm, then the right forearm to the right hand. Do the same with the left arm.

9 Slot the arms and legs into the correct shoulder and hip joints. Thread a ribbon or string through the tab at the top of the skull if you want your skeleton to dangle menacingly.

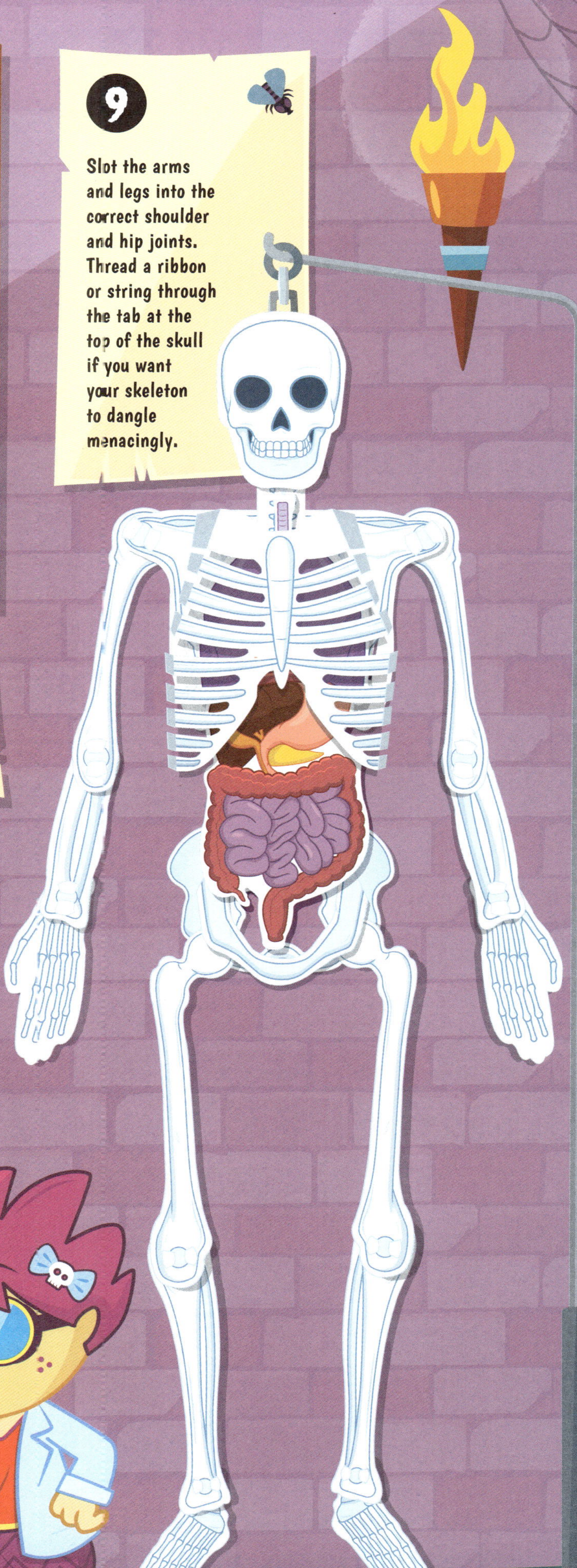

MUSCLE MONSTERS

You have over six hundred muscles in your body. A lot of them are used to move your skeleton around. Do some of these experiments to investigate how they work. Then turn the page upside down to discover the science behind your results.

Floating Arms

Stand inside a doorway and raise your arms from your sides, so you're pushing against the door frame. Push as hard as you can for one minute. Then step away from the door and relax your arms. Write down what you notice.

....

Muscle Measure

Do bigger muscles mean you're stronger? For this experiment, you need a few volunteers. Ask each volunteer to hold up a weight (a can of beans works well), bending their arm at the elbow. Measure around their upper arm, and write the measurement in the table below. Then ask them to lift up the weight by bending their arm at the elbow. Repeat until they can't do it any more. Keep count of how many lifts they manage, and write the result in the table.

Name of Volunteer	Upper arm measurement (cm)	Number of Lifts

There are two types of muscle movement—voluntary (where your brain tells your muscles to move) and involuntary (like sneezing or moving your hand away from a hot surface). Your muscles constantly work involuntarily to keep your limbs where they are. When you push the door frame, your brain overrides the involuntary signal with its own voluntary signal. If you keep pushing for a long time, then move away, your brain continues to override the signal for a little while, meaning your arms float up on their own!

Do bigger muscles mean you're stronger? The answer is, "often, but it depends." The that make up muscle can be denser and stronger in some people than others. Your brain makes a difference, too—the more you exercise, the more your brain learns to make all the cells in your muscles work at once, meaning you can get more power from each lift.

Tennis Menace

Do you think it's easier for your muscles to do one long squeeze, or lots of short ones? Test it with a tennis ball and a stopwatch. Squeeze the tennis ball as hard as you can, until you can't hold it any longer. Write down how many seconds you last. Do this with both hands, then let your hands rest. Then time yourself again, but this time, squeeze the tennis ball as hard as you can once per second until you can't continue. Write your results in the table.

Left hand: long squeeze	
Right hand: long squeeze	
Left hand: short squeezes	
Right hand: short squeezes	

Beat repeat

Find your pulse by putting two fingers (not your thumb) just under your jaw, to one side of your windpipe, and pressing lightly. You should feel a steady beat under your fingers. Use a stopwatch to measure one minute and count the number of beats. Write the number in the table below.

Then set your stopwatch for two minutes and do as many jumping jacks as you can. At the end of the two minutes, measure your pulse again for another minute and write the number in the second row of the table. What do you notice?

Before	
After	

You should find that your hand gets tired more quickly with the long squeeze. When you squeeze your hand, your muscles press on your blood vessels, so it's harder for your blood to bring fresh oxygen, which your muscles need to work. With short squeezes, your muscles actually help to push your blood along. But with both long and short squeezes, your muscles will get tired. The only muscle that doesn't get tired is your heart muscle, which is constantly squeezing and releasing.

Your heart beats to pump blood around your body. Your blood contains oxygen, which your muscles need to work. The more you make your muscles work, the more oxygen they need, so your heart has to beat more quickly to make sure they have enough.

HORRIBLE HAND

Your muscles are joined to your bones by stringy fibers called tendons. When your muscle contracts (squeezes), it pulls on the tendon, which in turn pulls on the bone. Use your press-out sheet to build this creepy articulated hand, complete with tendons, perfect for beckoning menacingly to lure victims to your lair.

You will need

- Your press-out sheet
- Glue
- That's it!

1 Press out the fingers one at a time. Carefully crease along all of the fold lines. Glue the tabs under the opposite side of each section to make four mini tubes along the length of each finger. (This bit is quite delicate!)

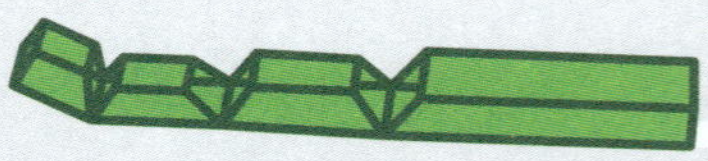

2 Take one finger and thread a tendon up through the little tube sections. Glue it to the tip of the shortest section. Repeat this with all four fingers.

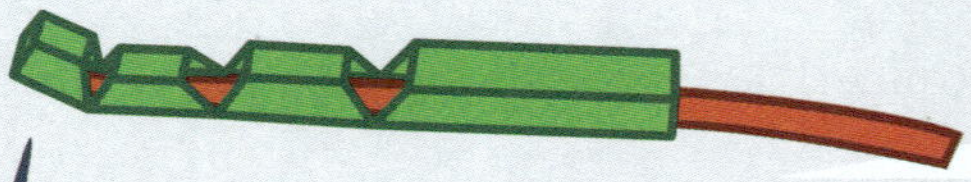

3 Lay out the fingers and glue them to make a right hand (if you want to make a left hand, turn the palm piece upside down and add the palm sticker from your sticker sheet to the white side).

4 Glue the palm piece into place, making sure it's securely attached to all four fingers.

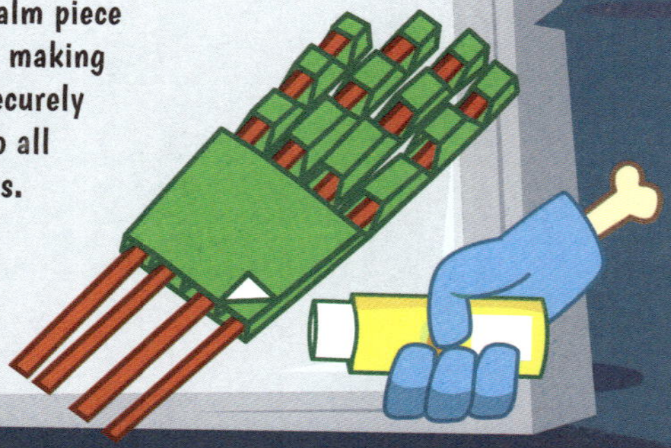

5 Build the thumb the same way as you built the fingers, gluing each of the tube sections. Thread the tendon through the thumb, gluing it at the tip of the shortest section.

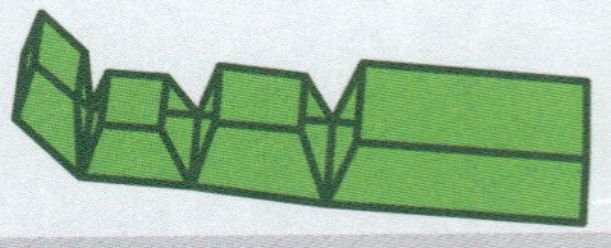

6 Glue the front of the thumb to the side of the index finger at a slight angle, so that if the back of the hand is lying flat against a table, the thumb points upwards at about a 30° angle.

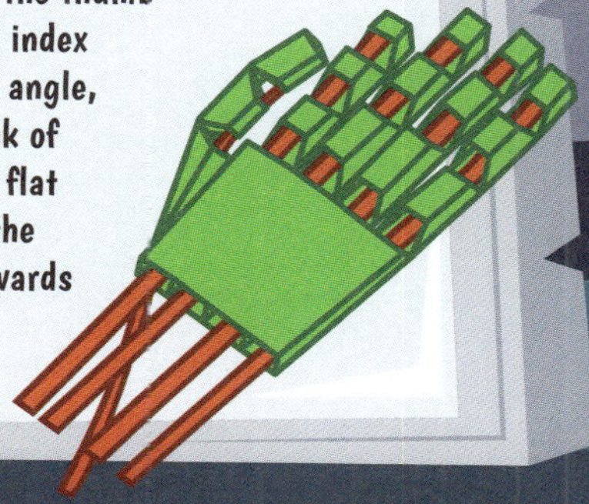

7 Arrange the fingers' tendons so that the fingers are lying flat and so the tendons are evenly spaced. Keep the thumb's tendon out of the way for the moment. Spread glue on the back of the glue tab and press it down onto the tendons to secure them.

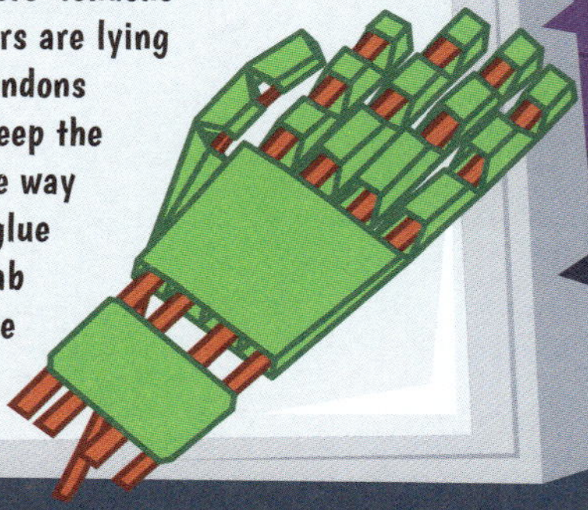

8 Pull the thumb's tendon onto the front of the pull tab, so it goes diagonally across the pull tab to the opposite corner. Glue it in place and cut off any excess tendon.

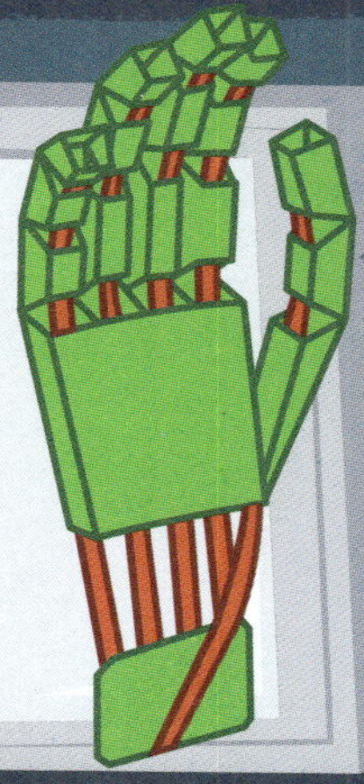

9 Pull the tab in different directions to make the fingers wiggle and move (cackling and yelling "it's alive!" are optional but encouraged).

WHAT DID THE ZOMBIE DO WHEN HE LOST A HAND?

WENT TO THE SECOND-HAND SHOP.

HOW DO YOU FIND A GRAVEYARD?

GO TO THE DEAD CENTER OF TOWN.

WHERE DID THE MONSTER KEEP HIS SPARE HAND?

IN A HANDBAG.

HOW DO YOU KNOW IF A GRAVEYARD IS POPULAR?

BECAUSE PEOPLE ARE DYING TO GET IN!

THE DIGESTIVE DINER

Food contains stuff your body needs to keep working, like protein from meat and beans, sugars from starchy foods like bread and rice, and vitamins from vegetables. Your disgusting digestive system breaks down big chunks of food into these tiny bits so your body can use them.

Dog's Dinner

Werewolf is chowing down on some gruesome grub. Use the stickers to put together his digestive system. Otherwise the food will just go straight through him. Prrp!

TEETH crush, chop, and grind food so you can swallow it.

SALIVA (or spit) mixes with your food, making it soggy. It also has chemicals in it that start to digest starchy food.

THE STOMACH is a bag of acidic juices. Muscles in the walls of the stomach squeeze and churn the food to mix it all up into a slurry.

THE ESOPHAGUS is a long tube that goes from your mouth to your stomach, lined with rippling muscles that push food along.

THE GALLBLADDER squirts out a liquid called bile that breaks up big globs of fat into smaller globs, making them easier for your body to take in.

THE PANCREAS is a factory for lots of different chemicals. Some of these help to break down protein and starchy food so your body can take them in.

THE SMALL INTESTINE is a long tube that picks up useful stuff from the slurry of food and dumps it into the blood, which carries it around the body to where it's needed.

THE LARGE INTESTINE squeezes out all the water from the mushy leftover food. By the time this mush reaches the end of the large intestine (the RECTUM), it's ready to be pooped out.

Digestion Demo

This sickening demonstration shows what happens to food as it passes through your digestive system. It's messy and truly vile. Perhaps you'd prefer to do a nicer, more wholesome activity instead, like making a daisy chain or singing a pleasant song? No? Well, you have been warned...

You will need

- 2 oz pineapple juice
- Banana and crackers
- Sealable plastic bag
- 3 paper cups
- Old nylon tights (ask permission first!)
- Large bowl
- Scissors

1 Pour the pineapple juice into the plastic bag. This represents the acidic juices in your stomach. Add the banana and the crackers—this represents swallowing some food. Add a couple of tablespoons of water to be your saliva.

2 Squish and churn the plastic bag until it's all mixed up into a horrible, mushy paste. In your body, this churning process can take up to five hours, but in this experiment a few minutes should be enough.

3 Cut off the base of a paper cup. Cut one leg off the tights, then stretch the cut end over the cup, so the cup makes a funnel. Hold the tights over a large bowl, then cut a hole in the plastic bag and pour the stomach contents into the tights.

4 Squeeze the tights hard to wring out the liquid. Muscles in the walls of your intestines squeeze the food gunk to wring out water and other good stuff so it can enter the rest of the body (the big bowl). In your body, this can take nearly two days!

5 When you've got as much liquid as possible out of the food mush, poke a thumb-sized hole in the bottom of the second paper cup to make your butt. Tip the mush from the tights into the cup.

6 To poop, push your last cup into the one that contains the mush. Watch in disgust as the waste material squeezes out of the paper cup's bottom. Truly, truly awful.

You probably shouldn't eat the fake poop (unless you're an actual rat).

LOATHSOME LUNGS

Your ghastly body needs a gas called oxygen from the air. As you breathe in, your lungs, the spongy bags in your chest, inflate with air. Your blood picks up oxygen from this air and carries it to where it's needed so your body can use it. Ghastly.

You will need

- 3 balloons
- Plastic drinks bottle
- 2 drinks straws
- strong sticky tape
- Plasticine/sticky tack

Bottle Breath

In your chest, you have a sheet of muscle under your lungs called your diaphragm. When this muscle contracts, it pulls down, making a larger space inside your chest. Air rushes into your lungs to fill this space.

Build a model of your breathing apparatus, with balloons for the lungs, a bottle for your chest, straws for your windpipe, and a flat piece of balloon to be your dire diaphragm.

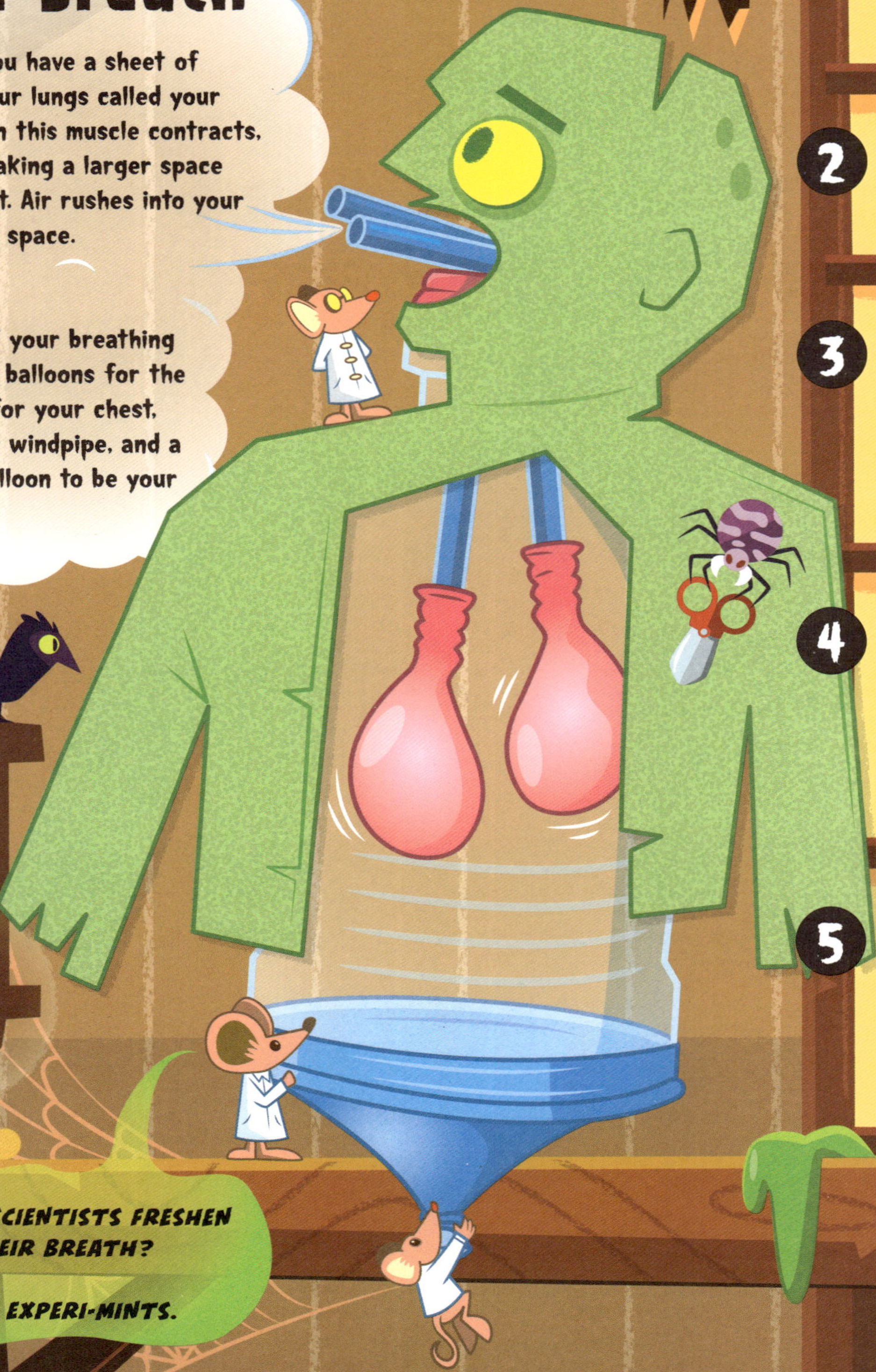

1. Tape a balloon to the end of each straw. Make sure you tape it tightly to make an airtight seal, without closing off the straws.
2. Tie a tight knot in the third balloon. Then use scissors to cut the balloon in half.
3. Ask an adult to cut the bottom off a plastic bottle. Then stretch the tied end of your cut balloon over the bottom of the bottle and tape it securely, making another airtight seal.
4. Take a ball of plasticine and poke a pencil through it. Feed the straw through the hole, then squish the plasticine around it to fill in the gaps, being careful not to close off the straw. Then take a second ball of plasticine and repeat this step with the other straw.
5. Push the two balls of plasticine together, then feed the straws into the top of the bottle. Use the plasticine to create a seal at the neck of the bottle. Pull down on the knot to make your lungs inflate.

HOW DO SCIENTISTS FRESHEN THEIR BREATH?

WITH EXPERI-MINTS.

Edible Snot

Snot. This gunky, goopy slime coats the inside of your nose and breathing tubes so bits of fluff and germs stick to it and get trapped. Then you cough or sneeze it out or, if you're a horrible monster, you pick it out of your schnozz and eat it. If you're not a monster, you may find this edible snot a lot more delicious.

You will need

- 3.5 oz boiling water
- 3 packs of lime gelatin powder
- 1.5 oz corn or fructose syrup
- Sugar sprinkles
- Metal tray

1. Pour the gelatin powder into a large bowl. Ask an adult to measure out the boiling water and add it to the gelatin powder.

2. Mix the gelatin powder into the water (get an adult to help with this until the gelatin has cooled down a bit).

3. Add the syrup to the gelatin. Mix it well. Then wait until the slime is cool enough to handle.

4. Pour the sprinkles out onto the metal tray. These are the germs trying to get into your lungs.

5. Use a spoon (or your hands) to scoop up the gelatin and try using it to pick up the sprinkles.

TOOT MONSTER

In your throat, you have two thin flaps called your vocal cords. Your voice works when air from your lungs is pushed through a very narrow gap between these vocal cords, making them vibrate noisily. Your mouth and tongue can shape this noise into words, laughter or a shriek of unimaginable terror, depending on the situation. This monster's voice works in much the same way as yours, with bellows to push air and a narrow gap for the air to pass through.

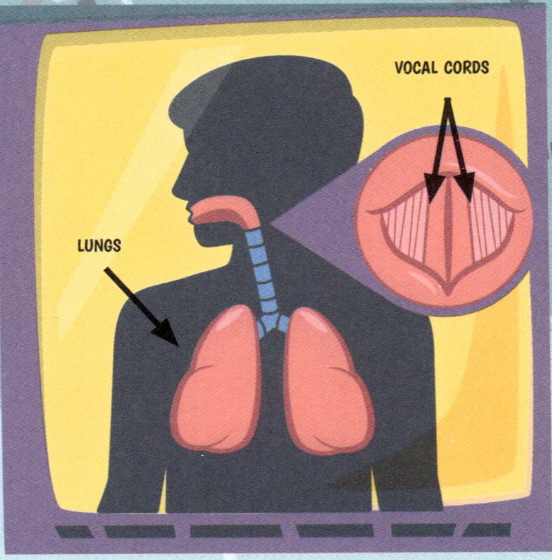

1 Press out the bellows of your monster. Pre-crease along all the score lines to make it easier to fold.

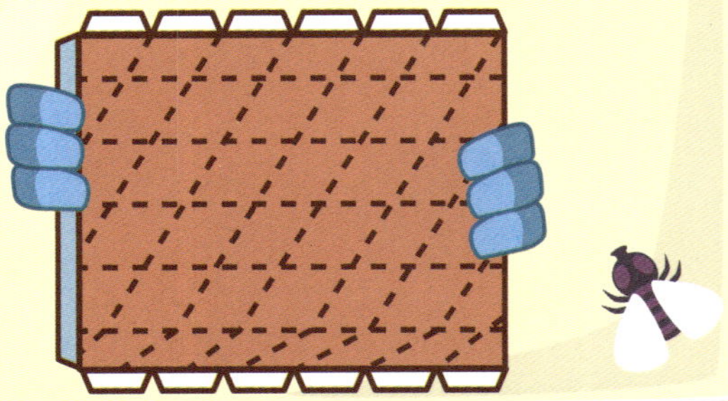

2 Roll the bellows into a tube shape and glue the flap down. Try to match up the lines as closely as possible. It may be easiest to do this around a rolling pin.

3 Starting at one end, fold along the crease lines of the bellows to make a concertina shape. Work your way down the bellows.

4 Fold up and glue the neck piece, leaving the tabs at the end free. Then fold up and glue the lower jaw.

5 Slot the neck piece into the lower jaw. Fold out the tabs at the top of the neck piece inside the bottom of the lower jaw. Use glue or sticky tape to secure the tabs.

6 Fold up and glue the head box. Glue the ears to either side and add the eye stickers onto the front of the head box.

7 Fit the head box into the lower jaw. There's no need to glue it into place. Leaving it unglued lets you move it around for the perfect whistle!

8 Glue the body base and feet onto the base of the bellows.

9 Glue the top of the body into place on the other side of the bellows.

10 Fit the neck into the hole in the body top to complete the model. Push the bellows up and down to make the monster toot!

BLOODY ORGANS

The horrible heart has the ghastly job of pumping blood all around the body, but it's not the only organ in the circulatory system. When building a monster, it is vital to make sure its blood visits all the organs in its circulatory system. Blood also needs to carry oxygen and chemicals to every single cell in its body. Otherwise, your undead monster will very quickly become a dead monster.

HOW DO YOU SPOT THE MOST POPULAR MONSTER ON VALENTINE'S DAY?

LOOK FOR THE ONE WHO'S STOLEN THE MOST HEARTS.

Blood Maze

Start at the blue arrow and follow the maze around the body, adding the organ stickers to the monster's body as you reach the correct area.

Brain

The brain uses more oxygen than any other part of the body, so it needs a constant supply of oxygen-rich blood.

Lungs

This is where the monster's blood picks up oxygen from the air he breathes in. All the cells in his body need a constant supply of oxygen in order to stay alive.

Heart

This pump has two parts. One side sends blood to the monster's lungs to pick up oxygen. The other, stronger side blasts this oxygen-rich blood all the way around the monster's terrifying body.

Liver

The liver cleans toxins from your monster's blood, breaking them down to stop harmful chemicals from building up inside his body. It then sends the waste products to the monster's digestive system so he can poop them out.

Spleen

The spleen recycles old red blood cells (the cells that carry oxygen) to make healthy new ones. It also stores spares of white blood cells that help you fight diseases, and platelets that form scabs if your monster cuts himself.

WHAT DO YOU CALL A ZOMBIE'S LIVER?

A DEAD-ER.

Kidneys

Your monster has two bean-shaped kidneys, which filter out extra water and waste products from your his blood to make pee.

BRAAAAINS

As well as being a delicious and nutritious snack for zombies, your brain is the control center for everything you do. It does all your thinking, feeling, and storing memories. It's a pretty clever organ.

Brain activity

Different parts, or lobes, of your brain are in charge of different things. All parts are working all of the time, but depending on what you're doing, one part might be working harder than the others. Use the color key to color in the zombie's brains to show which part of their brain they're using most.

Parts of the Brain (a zombie's tasting guide)

PROBLEM SOLVING
This is where the thinking happens. Tastes of homework with a hint of math.

SPEECH AND LANGUAGE
Talking, chatting, and gossiping all give this part of the brain a rather wordy aftertaste.

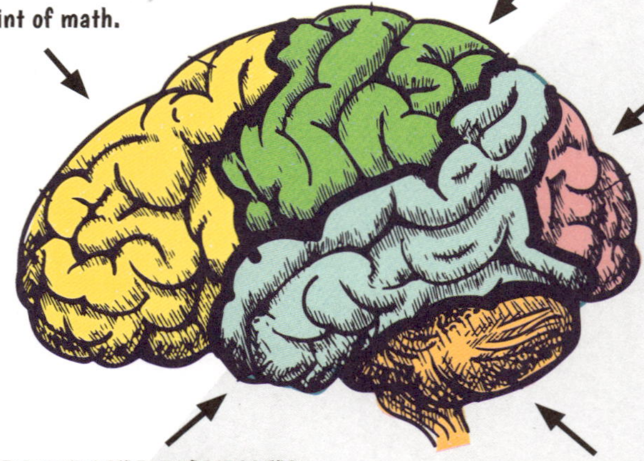

VISION
The area provides a video feed of the world. A small but juicy part of the brain.

PROCESSING EMOTIONS
Happiness, sadness, anger, and love all get managed here. Rather sweet, recommend saving for dessert.

BALANCE AND COORDINATION
A rather meaty section of the brain, due to it being constantly used to stop the body from falling over.

Memory quiz

Your brain is constantly making new memories. Test your brain's memory skills. Spend thirty seconds looking at the picture. Then cover up the rest of the page, and answer the questions below.

1. What color is the cat?

....

2. What time does the clock on the wall show?

....

3. How many spiders are crawling around the room?

3 7 11

3. Who's living in the jar above the fire?

Brian Auntie Vera Uncle George

4. How many bones is the blue zombie juggling?

....

STRANGE SENSES

Your senses tell your brain all about the world outside your body. You have five main senses: sight, smell, taste, hearing, and touch. Investigate them with some weird experiments.

Super Taster

Are you a super* taster? Find out by using a cotton ball to brush blue or green food coloring over your tongue. Cut a hole in a clean piece of wax paper with a hole punch. Place the piece with a hole in it on the front part of your tongue, then use a mirror and a magnifying glass (or ask a friend to help) to count the number of pink bumps you can see. Then use the table below to work out if you're a super taster.

Number of tastebuds	Taste level
1 – 10	Mildly sensitive taster
11 – 29	Moderately sensitive taster
30+	Super taster

*Despite the name, being a super taster may not be that super. Scientists say that super tasters find bitter tastes much stronger, which means they're less likely to enjoy vegetables like broccoli. They also find chili peppers hotter and fizzy drinks fizzier.

Who Nose?

Your nose notices smells, both nice and noxious. It also helps your tongue decide what it's tasting. Sound odd? See how much smell affects taste by getting some different flavored jelly beans.

Put a blindfold on (no peeking!) and get a friend to give you ten different jelly beans. Smell them one by one and guess what flavor they are, while your friend keeps a tally of how many you get correct. Then get your friend to give you ten more jelly beans. This time taste them and try to guess what flavor they are. Finally, repeat the test with another ten jelly beans, but this time hold your nose while you taste them. How many did you get correct this time?

	Number of correct guesses
Smell only	
Taste and smell	
Taste only	

Alarming Audio

Why did the scary monster have two ears? So its brain could work out what direction sounds were coming from. Did you think that was the start of a joke? Test this ability by asking a friend to set an alarm on a phone or alarm clock and hide it somewhere in the room. See how quickly you can track down the alarm. Then try it again, this time covering up one of your ears.

WHAT KIND OF MONSTER HAS THE BEST HEARING?

THE EERIEST ONE.

Touch Test

Just beneath your skin, you have billions of sensors that tell you if you're touching something, and if that something is hard, soft, hot, cold, or slimy. Some parts of your body, like your fingertips, have more of these sensors than other parts.

Test which bits of your body are best at sensing touch by unbending a paperclip, then bending it in half into a U shape, with the points about 1 cm apart. Put on a blindfold and ask a friend to lightly tap different parts of your body with either both points or one point of the paperclip without telling you which they're doing. Which parts of your body can you easily tell whether it's one point or two? Fill in your answers in the table below.

	Easy, medium, or difficult?
Finger tip	
Palm of hand	
Back of hand	
Forearm	
Upper arm	
Shoulder	
Sole of foot	
Back of calf	

Jumpin' Drum

Deep in your ear, you have a very thin, stretchy bit of skin called your eardrum. Sounds make waves or wobbles in the air. Your outer ear funnels these wobbles towards your eardrum. This makes your eardrum wobble in patterns that your brain understands as speech, music, or the haunting howl of the undead.

See how your eardrum works by cutting the top off a balloon and stretching it tightly over a bowl. Secure it with an elastic band and sprinkle some grains of rice on top. Then shout as loud as you can to make the rice dance and jump on top of the balloon.

Eye, Eye

Turn the page for some weird optical illusions.

SIGHT FRIGHT

Your senses send information to your brain as electrical signals that zap along your nerve cells. Your brain then unscrambles these electrical signals to make sense of them. It's usually pretty good at this, but sometimes it doesn't get it quite right. Try these experiments. You won't believe your eyes...

Optical Oddities

Optical illusions are pictures that are designed to trick your brain into seeing things that aren't really there. Try some for yourself!

a

What color are the spaces at the corners of the squares?

b

What can you see in the picture above? A vase or two faces?

c

Are the lines in this picture straight or curved?

d

Which flower has a larger middle?

Zombie Zoetrope

When your eyes see lots of images very quickly, your brain fills in the gaps to make a moving video. Without this ability, films would just look like a series of snapshots and the world would go black every time you blink. Instead your clever brain gets to enjoy monster movies in all their technicolor moving glory. Test it for yourself with this zoetrope—an old-fashioned moving image machine.

You will need

- Your press-out sheets
- An old CD or DVD
- Empty lip salve tube

1 Glue the two pieces of the zoetrope together into one long strip. Try to line up the edges as neatly as possible.

2 Fold the long strip over to make a mountain fold. Press out the long thin tabs at the top of the folded strip.

3 Curve the strip around into a circle shape, with the zombie pictures on the inside of the circle. Glue the tab inside the mountain fold so it's hidden. You may want to secure it with a clothespin until the glue dries.

4 Place the circle onto an old CD (ask a nearby grown-up's permission first). Use sticky tape to secure the CD around the bottom edge of zoetrope.

5 Wash up the old lip salve tube and let it dry. Take the lid off and put the top of it through the middle of the CD. The CD should balance on top of the lip salve tube.

6 Spin the CD to make the zoetrope spin. Peer through the gaps to see the lurching, shuffling zombie come to life.

HOW TO BUILD A BODY

If you don't have a handy supply of ready-made monster bits to build a monster from, don't worry! You can still build a monster from scratch, using the tiny cells that are the building blocks of all living things (including you). You'll only need a few billion cells to get started.

Cell Match

Cells are shaped differently depending on their jobs. Draw lines to match the cells to their descriptions. Then add stickers to the circles to show where in the body you would find the cells.

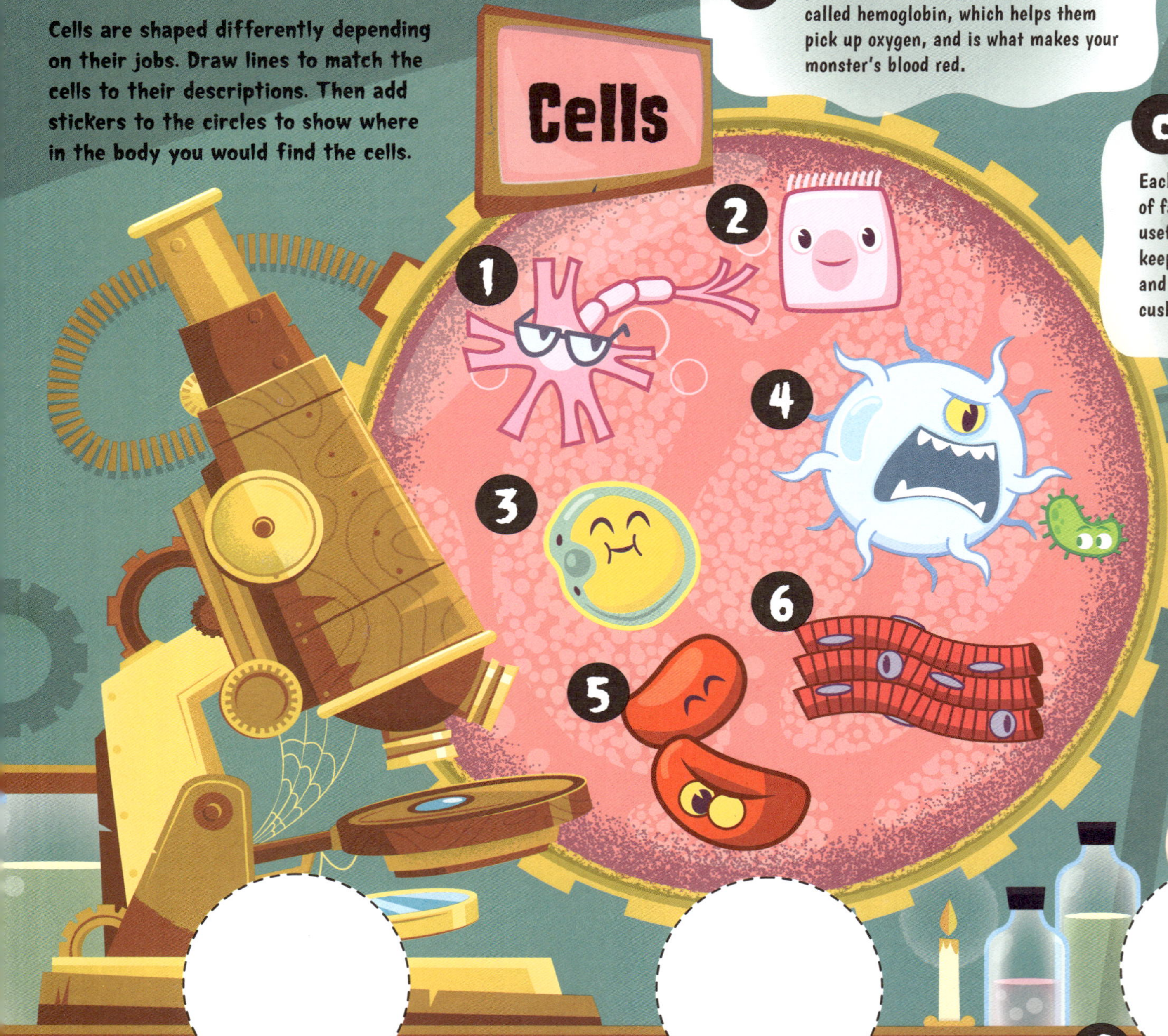

a Your monster's red blood cells are packed full of a bright red chemical called hemoglobin, which helps them pick up oxygen, and is what makes your monster's blood red.

b Your monster's white blood cells are great big cells that attack germs that enter the body.

c Each fat cell has a big blob of fat inside it. This fat is useful for storing energy, keeping your monster warm, and giving him a soft, cushioned bottom to sit on.

d The cells that line your monster's intestines have lots of tiny hairs called villi, that help your monster to absorb as much good stuff as possible from the food he eats.

e The nerve cells that carry messages around your monster's body have lots of branches, so they can pick up messages quickly, and a long tail so they can carry messages over long distances.

f Muscle cells are long thin fibers, tightly packed together into tight bundles. When lots of muscle cells bunch up at once, they're strong enough to move your monster's body around.

Disgusting DNA

Nearly every cell in your body contains DNA, the chemical blueprint for your body. Your DNA is unique to you, unless you have an identical twin or an army of clones. The first step in building your own personal army of clones is to extract your DNA, which you can do using some common household items.

You will need

- 1 T salt
- 3.5 oz ml water
- 1.5 oz ice-cold rubbing alcohol or vodka
- Food coloring
- Clear dish soap
- Pineapple juice
- Toothpick

1 Mix the salt and water, making sure all the salt is dissolved in the water and there isn't any left at the bottom of the jar.

2 Take a mouthful of the saltwater, BUT DON'T SWALLOW IT. Instead, swish and gargle it around your mouth.

3 After two minutes, spit the saltwater back into the glass. The saltwater will have picked up lots of the tiny cells that line the inside of your cheeks.

4 Add a few drops of dish soap and a few drops of pineapple juice. Carefully swish the cup to gently mix the liquid. Try not to cause any bubbles.

5 Add a few drops of food coloring to the rubbing alcohol/vodka. Carefully pour the alcohol into the saltwater mix, letting it trickle against the side of the glass. The alcohol should sit in a layer on top of the saltwater.

6 Wait one minute, then carefully dip the toothpick into the glass so that its tip is at the point where the saltwater and the alcohol join. Delicately swirl the toothpick around in one direction, then lift it out of the glass. You should see some stringy white stuff. This is millions of strands of your DNA all clumped together.

BODY DEFENSE

All of the different types of gunk and goo your face makes are barriers to stop germs from getting into your body. Earwax traps germs before they can get to your delicate ear drum and into your ear canal. Snot catches germs as you breathe them in and lets you cough or sneeze them out. Spit washes germs in your mouth down into your stomach, where the strong stomach acid can usually break them down. Tears flush the germs out of your eyes. But germs still don't give up that easily. Play this board game against a friend to battle germs against the body's gunky barriers.

You will need

- 2 dice
- Stickers
- Coins to make tokens

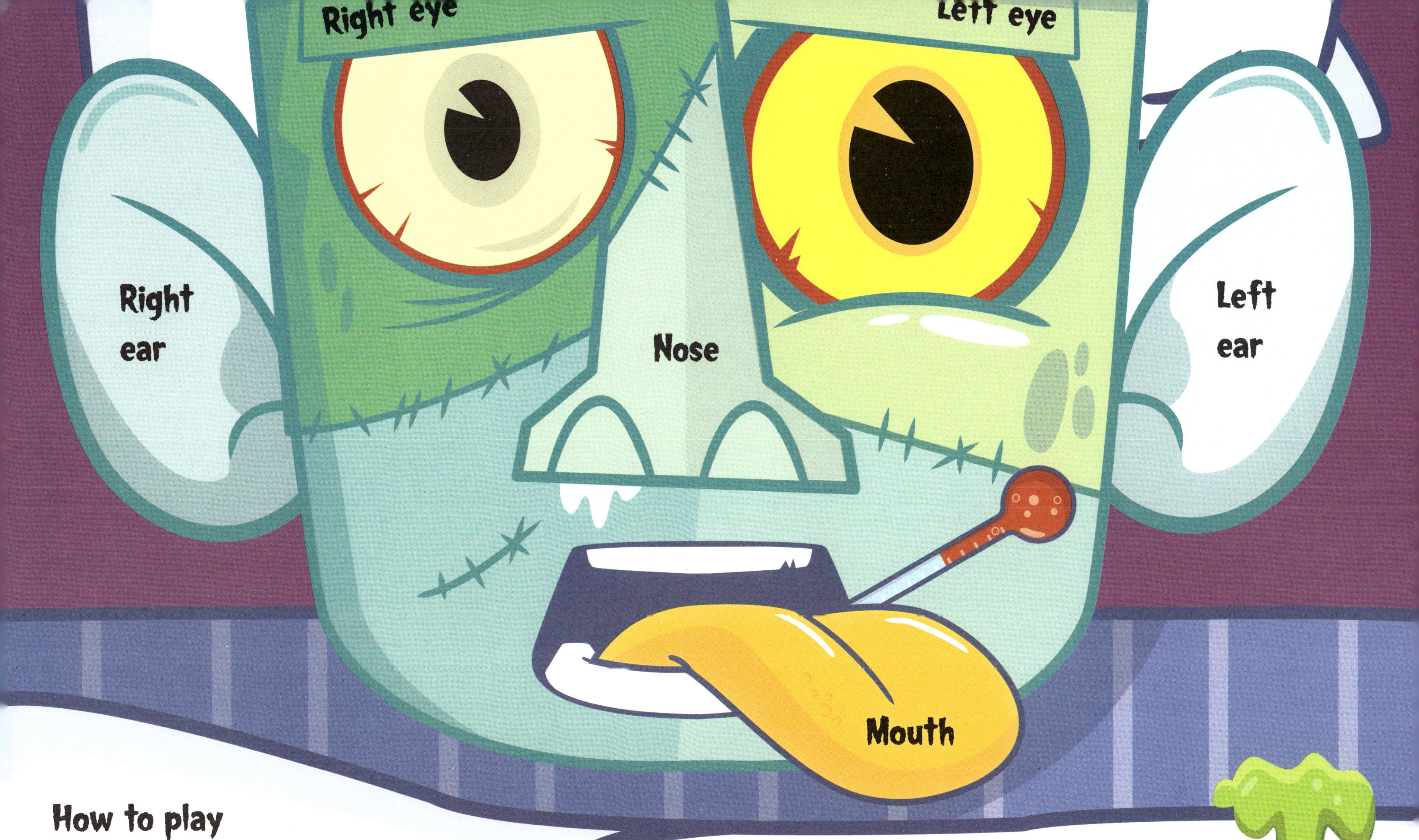

How to play

Make tokens by sticking the stickers onto coins. One player is the Body and takes all the snot, spit, tears, and earwax tokens. One player is the Germs and takes all the germ tokens. The Germs start by picking a "square" to try to infect out of the right eye, left eye, right ear, left ear, nose or mouth. Each player rolls a dice. Whoever gets the highest number puts their token on the square, either infecting it (the Germs) or protecting it (the Body). Players then take turns to pick a square to battle over. To battle, there must not currently be any tokens on the square. Players can use their turn to try to remove opponent's tokens from infected/protected squares by rolling their dice three times. For each six they roll, they remove one of their opponent's tokens. Players may also use their turn to add extra tokens to squares that they already have tokens on. They can do this by throwing the dice three times, and for every six they roll, they add a token to that square, up to a maximum of three tokens per square. Whoever gets a token on every

GERM WARFARE

If germs manage to get past the snot and the earwax and all the other barriers your body has, that doesn't mean they've won. Your blood is filled with cells whose job it is to fight off these mini monsters.

Who's Who?

Use the stickers to complete the lineup of Defenders vs Germs.

The Defenders

These cells, known as white blood cells, all have different jobs to keep the invaders at bay.

a

Neutro Phil, a neutrophil, destroys enemy germs by swallowing them. Om nom nom.

b

Bea Cell, a B cell, fires antibodies to help other cells recognize invading bacteria and infected cells, and to immobilize viruses.

c

T-Cell, a T cell, patrols the body looking for infected cells to kill, as well as keeping a record of the diseases the immune system has met before, so they can fight them faster next time.

d

Mo Nosite, a monocyte, is the trash collector of the body. When the other cells have done their jobs, Mo cleans up the mess.

The Invaders

These are the mini monsters who can make you sick. There are three main types:

e

Bacteria are single cells that feed off the sugary soup inside your body. Many have straggly tails or tiny rippling hairs to let them swim around inside your body. Some bacteria are friendly and help you digest food. Others can make you sick.

f

Viruses try to invade your cells and turn them into factories to make more viruses. Lots of viruses, like cold and flu viruses, have lumpy coats covered in prongs. These prongs help them bind to your cells, but they also make an easy way for your white cells to recognize them.

g

Parasites are living creatures that latch onto another living thing, feeding off them like tiny vampires. Lice, worms, and mites are all types of parasites.

Antibody Cannon

Be like a B cell! Fire off antibodies to knock down invading germs with this bacteria-blasting cannon. How many can you knock down in one go?

You will need

- Your press-out sheets
- Empty toilet paper roll
- 2 balloons
- Paper clip
- Table tennis ball
- Sticky tape

1 Build your B cell out of the press-out sheets, gluing the tabs to their matching sides.

2 Tie a knot in a balloon, then cut it in half. You can discard the top half, or use it for the model ear on p24.

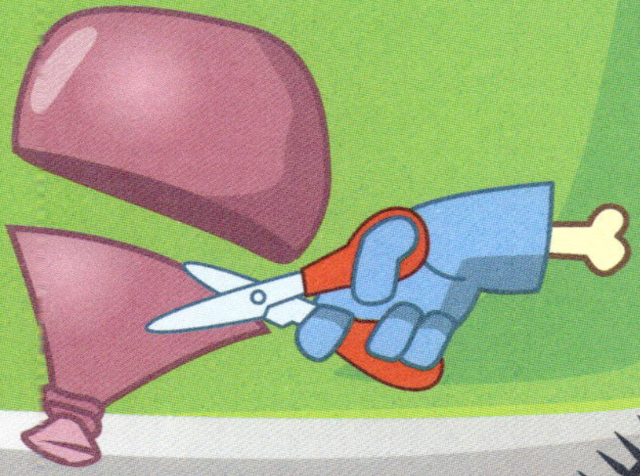

3 Use sticky tape to attach the balloon to the toilet paper roll. Try to make the seal as strong and airtight as possible.

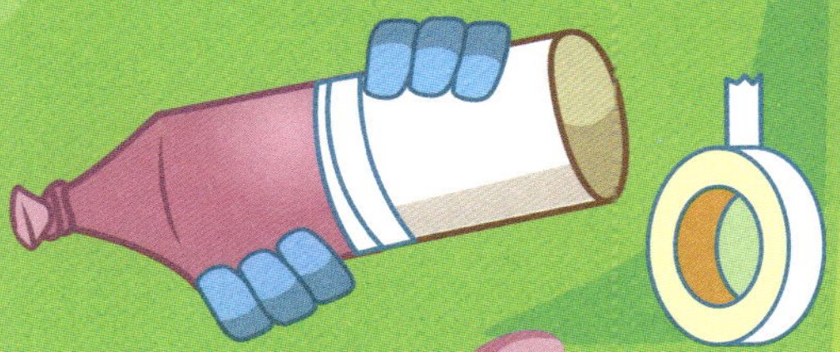

4 Slot the toilet paper roll into the B cell so it sticks out at one end. Attach it with sticky tape.

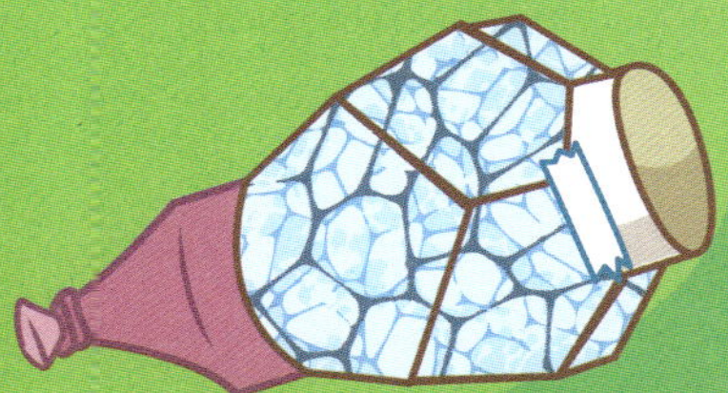

5 The toilet paper roll should be the correct width to fit the table tennis ball. Put the table tennis ball inside the tube.

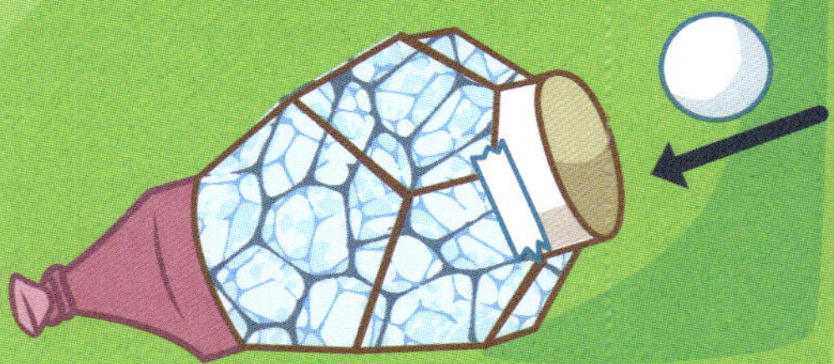

6 Press out the body invaders and slot them into their bases so they stand up. Pull back the knot of the balloon, then release suddenly to fire the table tennis ball at the invaders.

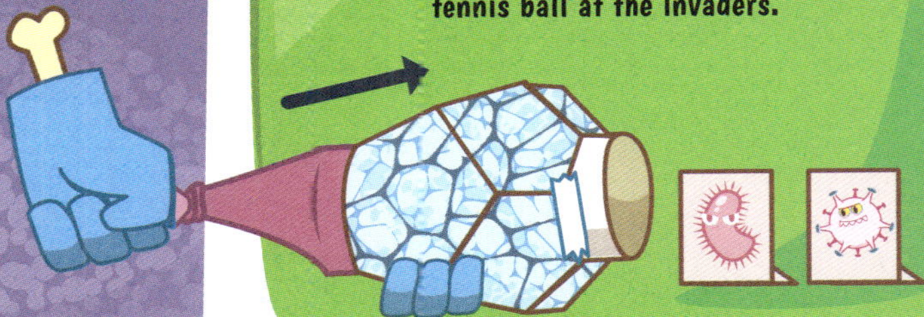

HISTORY OF MEDICINE

Luckily, when your body's defenses don't manage to fight off an infection, modern medicine is there to help. It's taken thousands of years to get to that point, though.

Do NOT try these at home!

Cure or Kill

People through history had some strange ideas about how to cure diseases. Some of these have been tested and developed by doctors into cures that we use today. Others, thankfully, have been left deep in the past. All of these cures were used by people through history. Add a lab rat sticker to the cures that are still used, in one form or another, by real doctors today. Add a skull to the ones left in the past where they belong.

a Putting maggots onto a wound was a battlefield cure in various wars through history.

Cure or kill?

b People tried a lot of cures for the Great Plague. One of the weirdest was strapping a chicken to the sores that developed under the sufferer's armpits.

Cure or kill?

c In the late 1800s, people would swallow tiny amounts of dynamite to treat chest pain.

Cure or kill?

d A medieval cure for burns was to allow snails to slither over the wound.

Cure or kill?

e If an Anglo Saxon had sore eyes, they could try tying a live crab around their neck.

Cure or kill?

f

From the Stone Age, people drilled holes in their heads to cure headaches.

Cure or kill?

g

Thousands of years ago, in ancient Egypt, people would pour honey on their wounds to help them heal.

Cure or kill?

h

Rich Romans treated headaches by soaking a chameleon in wine, then sprinkling the wine on their heads.

Cure or kill?

i

Poor Romans would cure their headaches by chewing on willow bark.

Cure or kill?

j

Tudors would tie a dead mouse onto their faces to remove warts.

Cure or kill?

WHY ARE GHOSTS SUCH BAD LIARS?

YOU CAN SEE RIGHT THROUGH THEM.

ANSWERS

Pages 2–3: Spooky Skeletons

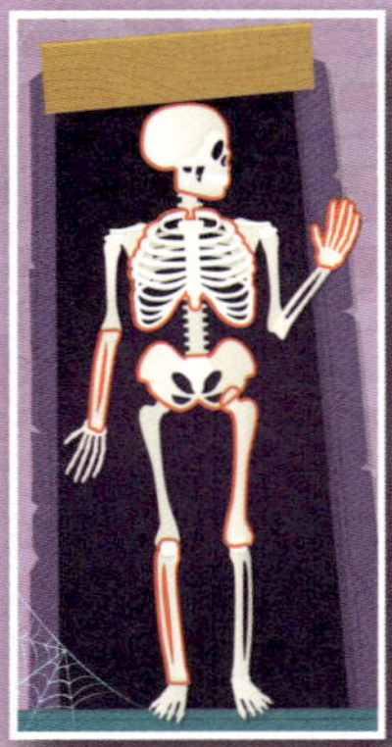

Pages 10–11: The Digestive Diner

Pages 16–17: Bloody Organs

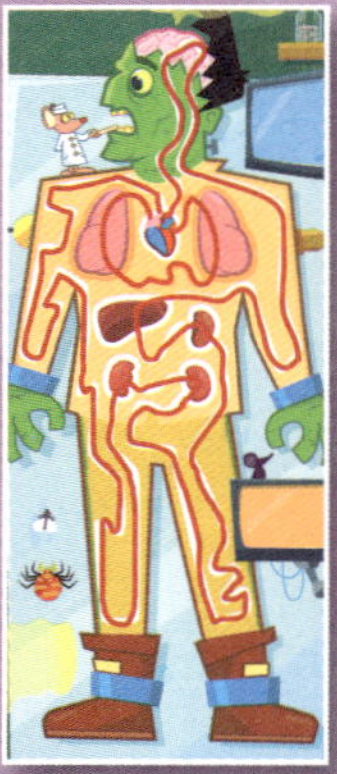

Pages 18–19: Braaaains

Memory quiz

1. The cat is grey/black.
2. The clock is showing 8 o'clock.
3. There are 7 spiders crawling around.
4. Auntie Vera
5. The blue zombie is juggling 5 bones.

Pages 22–23: Sight Fright

a. The spaces at the corners of the squares are white (not gray as they may look!)
b. People may see just the faces, just the vase, or both.
c. The lines are all straight. You can use a ruler to check.
d. The circles in the middle of both flowers are the same size.

Pages 24–25: How to Build a Body

a - 5 b - 4 c - 3 d - 2 e - 1 f - 6

Pages 28–29: Germ Warfare

Pages 30–31: History of Medicine

a. Cure. Specially disinfected maggots eat the infected flesh and leave the healthy flesh untouched. They also ooze an antibacterial goo, which helps to clean the wound.
b. Kill.
c. Cure. Nitroglycerin, the explosive chemical in dynamite, is used to treat heart attacks.
d. Cure. The slime from snails can be cleaned in a lab and used as a soothing ointment to help heal burns.
e. Kill.
f. Cure (very rarely). In extreme circumstances, such as a major brain injury or a stroke, a part of the skull may be removed to relieve pressure on the brain.
g. Cure. Honey is antiseptic, and may speed up healing in minor wounds.
h. Kill. You still have a headache, but now you have an angry chameleon, too.
i. Cure. Willow bark contains a chemical called salicylic acid that has been used to develop acetylsalicylic acid, the active ingredient in aspirin.
j. Kill. And pretty icky.

Your Skeleton pages 2-3

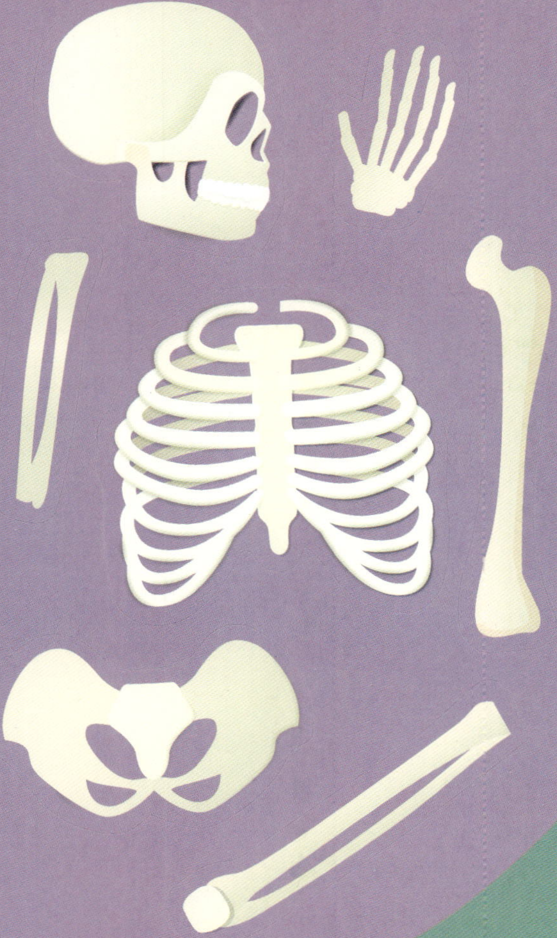

Dog's dinner

pages 10-11

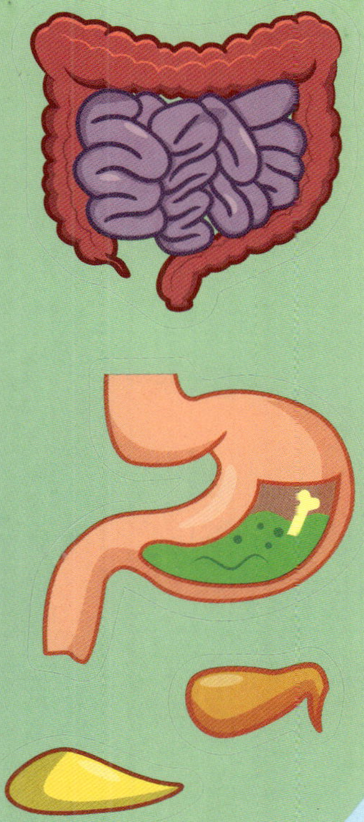

Blood maze pages 16-17

Cell match

pages 24-25

Who's who? pages 28-29

Who's who?

pages 28-29

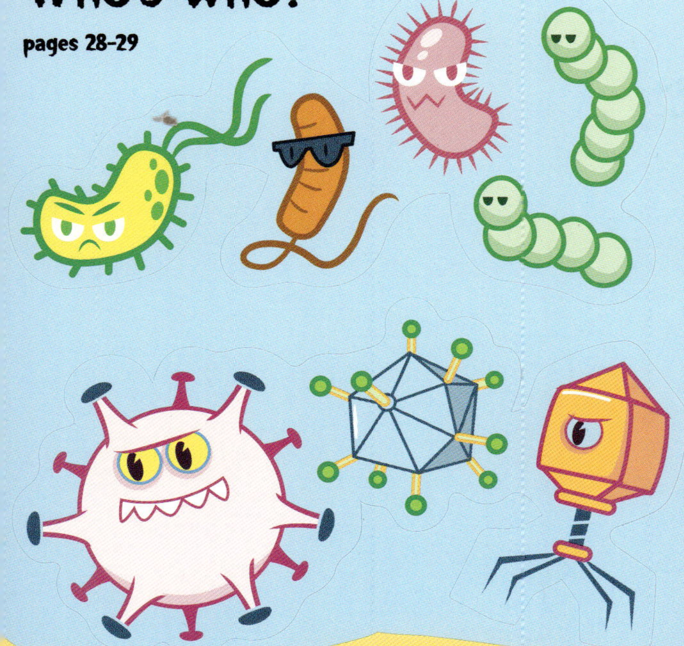

Body defence

pages 26-27

Horrible Hand Press-out

Left hand palm

pages 8-9

Kill or cure

pages 30-31

Toot monster eyes

pages 14-15